core belief™

Bible Study Series
for senior high

WHY
Prayer
MATTERS

Group

Loveland, Colorado

Why Prayer Matters

Core Belief Bible Study Series

Credits

Editors: Helen Turnbull and Michael D. Warden
Creative Development Editor: Paul Woods
Chief Creative Officer: Joani Schultz
Copy Editor: Candace McMahan
Art Director: Ray Tollison
Cover Art Director: Jeff A. Storm
Cover Photographer: Craig DeMartino
Computer Graphic Artist: Eris Klein
Photographer: Jafe Parsons
Production Manager: Gingar Kunkel

ISBN 0-7644-0893-3

10 9 8 7 6 5 4 3 2 1   07 06 05 04 03 02 01 00 99 98

Printed in the United States of America.

core belief

Bible Study Series
for senior high

contents:

the Core Belief: Prayer

Simply put, prayer is honest communication with God. It's how we build a personal relationship with our Creator, Redeemer, Father, and Friend. It's a way of life and involves our entire being. More than just words we say at a specified time of day, it's how we live our lives in constant contact with God. We can pray about anything, using a variety of means to communicate with God. We can pray by ourselves or in the company of our brothers and sisters. We can pray in Jesus' name and with the Holy Spirit's power.

And when we pray, God responds. He hears our prayers, and we can trust that he answers our prayers wisely and lovingly.

the Helpful Stuff

the ▼Studies

▼Prayer as a Core Christian Belief

If your youth group is like most, only three out of every ten kids pray daily. Even fewer—a paltry fifteen percent—regard personal prayer as an important influence in their lives. Kids are still forming and deepening significant relationships—just not with the personal God of the universe. In addition, those who don't consider prayer a vital influence do not live in a vacuum. They're still affected by the media, popular culture, and the opinions of teachers and friends.

Fortunately, the news is not all bad: Ninety percent of kids express interest in learning how to pray. Nine out of every ten members of your youth group want to pray more often and more effectively. The door is wide open, so you can seize the opportunity and help your young people meet their most crucial need and desire, a vital relationship with their loving God.

Whether or not your kids know **teenage runaways,** they've all experienced the misery of feeling alone. The first study will teach your kids about runaways and perhaps prevent them from seeking a similar escape by showing them that God is always ready to listen.

Do your students really know the power of **prayer,** or are they just going through the motions? Teach them that prayer is important because God always answers their prayers. And use this second study to help students identify with others' comments on prayer to expose and relieve their doubts.

We all have our own special ways to pray. That's what makes prayer so personal. That's how we know prayer builds the trusting relationship we have with God. Use the third study to show kids that they can make their prayers personal, trusting, and even fun. What's important is how they develop a prayer life that includes **trusting God.**

The fourth study approaches the concept of **fasting** and how it fits in the life of today's Christian. Teach your kids that fasting is not about tradition or doctrine or food. Fasting, as well as other forms of prayer, is about how we need to focus on God.

When your kids discover that prayer is simply honest communication with our loving, personal God, they'll pray more often and with greater confidence. As a result, they'll love God more deeply and serve him more effectively in every area of their lives.

For a more comprehensive look at this Core Christian Belief, read Group's **Get Real: Making Core Christian Beliefs Relevant to Teenagers.**

DEPTHFINDER

HOW THE BIBLE DESCRIBES PRAYER

To help you effectively guide your kids toward this Core Christian Belief, use these overviews as a launching point for a more in-depth study of prayer.

● **Prayer includes honest communication and personal fellowship with God.** Prayer is more than just talking to God. It is relating openly and honestly to God as our closest and most faithful friend (Psalms 10; 18:1; Romans 8:14-16; and Hebrews 4:14-16).

● **Prayer is more a lifestyle than a momentary act.** Since God is always with us, we can and should communicate with him all the time. In short, our lives should be never-ending conversations with God (Psalm 55:16-17; Luke 18:1; Ephesians 6:18; and 1 Thessalonians 5:17).

● **Prayer involves the entire person.** Because prayer is our means of relating to and communicating with God, it must be more than a mindless repetition of pious words. Authentic prayer requires the full engagement of one's intellect, emotions, and will (Deuteronomy 6:5; 1 Samuel 1:9-11; Matthew 6:7; Colossians 4:2; and James 5:16).

● **We can pray to God about anything.** God is the sovereign and all-powerful ruler of the universe, so there is no problem too difficult for him. And since God loves us and lives within us, we can trust him to take seriously even our most minor concerns (Psalms 103:13-14; 113:4-9; Matthew 7:7-11; Romans 8:26-27; and Philippians 4:6).

● **There are as many types of prayer as there are types of people and circumstances.** In the Bible God authorizes many kinds of prayer, including complaint, praise, petition, thanksgiving, confession, intercession, expression of trust, and simply sharing thoughts and emotions (Psalms 13; 30; 51; Matthew 6:9-13; and 1 Timothy 2:1-4).

● **When we pray, we should trust that God will respond in a wise and loving way.** God accepts even a simple cry for help as an expression of trust in him. The only sign of a total lack of faith is the refusal to pray (Psalms 56:1-4; 62; Matthew 7:9-11; and Mark 9:24; 11:24).

- **The only inappropriate prayer is a dishonest or insincere prayer.** Since healthy relationships require honest communication, God wants us to express even negative thoughts and emotions. God knows when we're angry, confused, afraid, or weak in faith, and he loves us anyway. God wants us to talk honestly with him and rely upon him to get us through difficult times (Psalm 88; Jeremiah 20:7-18; Matthew 6:7; and Luke 18:9-14).

- **God answers our appeals in a variety of ways.** Sometimes God gives us what we ask for; other times he enables us to answer our own requests. Sometimes God asks us to wait or accept a response different from what we had asked for. In each instance, however, God acts wisely and lovingly (Luke 18:1-8 and 2 Corinthians 12:1-10).

- **We should pray with others and by ourselves.** When we join others in prayer, we draw closer to God and to one another. However, sometimes we should pray privately in order to develop our private relationships with God and avoid the temptation to call attention to ourselves (Psalm 74; 1 Kings 8:22-53; Matthew 6:5-6; and Acts 2:42; 4:24).

- **We should pray to God in the name of Jesus and the power of the Holy Spirit.** Since Jesus enables us to live in fellowship with God, we can rely on him when we approach God in prayer. The Holy Spirit helps us speak to and hear from God (John 15:7, 16; 16:23-24; Romans 8:26-27; and Ephesians 5:19-20).

CORE CHRISTIAN BELIEF OVERVIEW

Here are the twenty-four Core Christian Belief categories that form the backbone of Core Belief Bible Study Series:

The Nature of God	Jesus Christ	The Holy Spirit
Humanity	Evil	Suffering
Creation	The Spiritual Realm	The Bible
Salvation	Spiritual Growth	Personal Character
God's Justice	Sin & Forgiveness	The Last Days
Love	The Church	Worship
Authority	Prayer	Family
Service	Relationships	Sharing Faith

Look for Group's Core Belief Bible Study Series books in these other Core Christian Beliefs!

about

core belief

Bible Study Series
for senior high

Think for a moment about your young people. When your students walk out of your youth program after they graduate from junior high or high school, what do you want them to know? What foundation do you want them to have so they can make wise choices?

You probably want them to know the essentials of the Christian faith. You want them to base everything they do on the foundational truths of Christianity. Are you meeting this goal?

If you have any doubt that your kids will walk into adulthood knowing and living by the tenets of the Christian faith, then you've picked up the right book. All the books in Group's Core Belief Bible Study Series encourage young people to discover the essentials of Christianity and to put those essentials into practice. Let us explain...

What Is Group's Core Belief Bible Study Series?

Group's Core Belief Bible Study Series is a biblically in-depth study series for junior high and senior high teenagers. This Bible study series utilizes four defining commitments to create each study. These "plumb lines" provide structure and continuity for every activity, study, project, and discussion. They are:

● **A Commitment to Biblical Depth**—Core Belief Bible Study Series is founded on the belief that kids not only *can* understand the deeper truths of the Bible but also *want* to understand them. Therefore, the activities and studies in this series strive to explain the "why" behind every truth we explore. That way, kids learn principles, not just rules.

● **A Commitment to Relevance**—Most kids aren't interested in abstract theories or doctrines about the universe. They want to know how to live successfully right now, today, in the heat of problems they can't ignore. Because of this, each study connects a real-life need with biblical principles that speak directly to that need. This study series finally bridges the gap between Bible truths and the real-world issues kids face.

● **A Commitment to Variety**—Today's young people have been raised in a sound bite world. They demand variety. For that reason, no two meetings in this study series are shaped exactly the same.

● **A Commitment to Active and Interactive Learning**—Active learning is learning by doing. Interactive learning simply takes active learning a step further by having kids teach each other what they've learned. It's a process that helps kids internalize and remember their discoveries.

For a more detailed description of these concepts, see the section titled "Why Active and Interactive Learning Works With Teenagers" beginning on page 57.

So how can you accomplish all this in a set of four easy-to-lead Bible studies? By weaving together various "power" elements to produce a fun experience that leaves kids challenged and encouraged.

THE ISSUE: Relationships

Betrayed!

HELPING KIDS DEAL WITH REJECTION FROM THE PEOPLE THEY LOVE

by Jennifer Carrell

THE POINT:

God is love.

■ Betrayal has very little shock value for this generation. It's as commonplace as compact discs and mosh pits. For many kids today, betrayal characterizes their parents' wedding vows. It's part of their curriculum at school; it defines the headlines and evening news. Betrayal is not only accepted—it's expected. ■ At the heart of such acceptance lies the belief that nothing is absolute. No vow, no law, no promise can be trusted. Relationships are betrayed at the earliest convenience. Repeatedly, kids see that something called "love" lasts just as long as it's [convenient.] ...permanence. But deep inside, they hunger to see a

The Study
AT A GLANCE

SECTION	MINUTES	WHAT STUDENTS WILL DO	SUPPLIES
Discussion Starter	up to 5	JUMP-START—Identify some of the most common themes in today's movies.	Newsprint, marker
Investigation of Betrayal	12 to 15	REALITY CHECK—Form groups to compare anonymous, real-life stories of betrayal with experiences in their own lives.	"Profiles of Betrayal" handouts (p. 20), highlighter pens, newsprint, marker, tape
	3 to 5	WHO BETRAYED WHOM?—Guess the identities of the people profiled in the handouts.	Paper, tape, pen
Investigation of True Love	15 to 18	SOURCE WORK—Study and discuss God's definition of perfect love.	Bibles, newsprint, marker
	5 to 7	LOVE MESSAGES—Create unique ways to send a "message of love" to the victims of betrayal they've been studying.	Newsprint, markers, tape
Personal Application	10 to 15	SYMBOLIC LOVE—Give a partner a personal symbol of perfect love.	Paper lunch sack, pens, scissors, paper, catalogs

notes:

● **A Relevant Topic**—More than ever before, kids live in the now. What matters to them and what attracts their hearts is what's happening in their world at this moment. For this reason, every Core Belief Bible Study focuses on a particular hot topic that kids care about.

● **A Core Christian Belief**—Group's Core Belief Bible Study Series organizes the wealth of Christian truth and experience into twenty-four Core Christian Belief categories. These twenty-four headings act as umbrellas for a collection of detailed beliefs that define Christianity and set it apart from the world and every other religion. Each book in this series features one Core Christian Belief with lessons suited for junior high or senior high students.

"But," you ask, "won't my kids be bored talking about all these spiritual beliefs?" No way! As a youth leader, you know the value of using hot topics to connect with young people. Ultimately teenagers talk about issues because they're searching for meaning in their lives. They want to find the one equation that will make sense of all the confusing events happening around them. Each Core Belief Bible Study answers that need by connecting a hot topic with a powerful Christian principle. Kids walk away from the study with something more solid than just the shifting ebb and flow of their own opinions. They walk away with a deeper understanding of their Christian faith.

● **The Point**—This simple statement is designed to be the intersection between the Core Christian Belief and the hot topic. Everything in the study ultimately focuses on The Point so that kids study it and allow it time to sink into their hearts.

● **The Study at a Glance**—A quick look at this chart will tell you what kids will do, how long it will take them to do it, and what supplies you'll need to get it done.

The Bible Connection—This is the power base of each study. Whether it's just one verse or several chapters, The Bible Connection provides the vital link between kids' minds and their hearts. The content of each Core Belief Bible Study reflects the belief that the true power of God—the power to expose, heal, and change kids' lives—is contained in his Word.

THE POINT OF *BETRAYED!*:

God is love.

THE BIBLE CONNECTION

1 JOHN 4:7-21 | The Apostle John explains the nature and definition of perfect love.

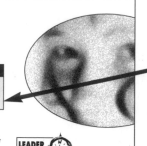

I n this study, kids will compare the imperfect love defined in real-life stories of betrayal to God's definition of perfect love.

By making this comparison, kids can discover that God is love and therefore incapable of betraying them. Then they'll be able to recognize the incredible opportunity God offers to experience the only relationship worthy of their absolute trust.

Explore the verses in The Bible Connect mation in the Depthfinder boxes throughou understanding of how these Scriptures con

LEADER TIP for The Study

THE STUDY

DISCUSSION STARTER ▼

Jump-Start (up to 5 minutes) As kids arrive, ask them to thi common themes in movies, books, TV show have kids each contribute ideas for a mas two other kids in the room and sharing their their suggestions, while their responses on ne **come up with a lot of great id s. Even th ent, look through this list an try to disc ments most of these theme have in com

After kids make several su gestions, menti responses are connected h the idea of be

● **Why do you think etrayal is such a**

Betrayed! **17**

LEADER TIP for The Study

Because this topic can be so powerful and relevant to kids' lives, your group members may be tempted to get caught up in issues and lose sight of the deeper biblical principle found in The Point. Help your kids grasp The Point by guiding kids to focus on the biblical investigation and discussing how God's truth connects with reality in their lives.

DEPTHFINDER UNDERSTANDING INTEGRITY

Y our students may not be entirely familiar with the meaning of integrity, especially as it might apply to God's character in the Trinity. Use these definitions (taken from Webster's II New Riverside Dictionary) and other information to help you guide kids toward a better understanding of how God maintains integrity through the three expressions of the Trinity.

Integrity: 1. Firm adherence to a code or standard of values. 2. The state of being unimpaired. 3. The quality or condition of being undivided.

Synonyms for integrity include probity, completeness, wholeness, soundness, and perfection.

Our word "integrity" comes from the Latin word *integritas*, which means soundness. *Integritas* is also the root of the word "integer," which means "whole or complete," as in a "whole" number.

The Hebrew word that's often translated "integrity" (for example, in Psalm 25:21 [NIV]) is *tom*. It means whole, perfect, sincere, and honest.

CREATIVE GOD-EXPLORATION ▼

Top Hats (18 to 20 minutes) Form three groups, with each trio member from the previous activity going to a different group. Give each group Bibles, paper, and pens, and assign each group a different hat God wears: Father, Son, or Holy Spirit. their goal is to write one list describing what God does in the God's character

---

Depthfinder Boxes—These informative sidelights located throughout each study add insight into a particular passage, word, historical fact, or Christian doctrine. Depthfinder boxes also provide insight into teen culture, adolescent development, current events, and philosophy.

Holy Profiles

Your assigned Bible passage describes how a particular person or group responded when confronted with God's holiness. Use the information in your passage to help your group discuss the questions below. Then use your flashlights to teach the other two groups what you discover.

■ Based on your passage, what does holiness look like?

■ What does holiness sound like?

■ When people see God's holiness, how does it affect them?

■ How is this response to God's holiness like humility?

■ Based on your passage, how would you describe humility?

■ Why is humility an appropriate human response to God's holiness?

■ Based on what you see in your passage, do you think you are a humble person? Why or why not?

■ What's one way you could develop humility in your life this week?

● **Leader Tips**—These handy information boxes coach you through the study, offering helpful suggestions on everything from altering activities for different-sized groups to streamlining discussions to using effective discipline techniques.

● **Handouts**—Most Core Belief Bible Studies include photocopiable handouts to use with your group. Handouts might take the form of a fun game, a lively discussion starter, or a challenging study page for kids to take home—anything to make your study more meaningful and effective.

The Last Word on Core Belief Bible Studies

Soon after you begin to use Group's Core Belief Bible Study Series, you'll see signs of real growth in your group members. Your kids will gain a deeper understanding of the Bible and of their own Christian faith. They'll see more clearly how a relationship with Jesus affects their daily lives. And they'll grow closer to God.

But that's not all. You'll also see kids grow closer to one another.

That's because this series is founded on the principle that Christian faith grows best in the context of relationship. Each study uses a variety of interactive pairs and small groups and always includes discussion questions that promote deeper relationships. The friendships kids will build through this study series will enable them to grow *together* toward a deeper relationship with God.

• While you're teaching this class, nearly 150 teenagers will run away from home.

The Diary of Teenage Runaways

by Jane Vogel

THE POINT:

God is always ready to listen.

■ While you're teaching this class, nearly 150 teenagers will run away from home. ■ That adds up to nearly 1.3 million American teenagers who run away each year. Although their "surface" reasons vary, one underlying cause remains constant: Kids feel their parents aren't listening to them. ■ This study focuses on the reasons kids leave home, recognizes the feelings of isolation and loneliness that all young people share, and helps point teenagers to their heavenly Father—who's always ready to listen.

The Study
AT A GLANCE

SECTION	MINUTES	WHAT STUDENTS WILL DO	SUPPLIES
Focusing Time	5 to 10	RUNNING HOME?—Play a game that helps them imagine what it would be like to run away from home.	Masking tape, small rubber ball
Runaway Journey	35 to 45	ON THE RUN—Form groups to explore reasons kids run away and discover how God responds to runaways of all kinds.	"Runaway" handouts (pp. 21-24), masking tape, small notebooks, pens, Bibles
Personal Application	5 to 10	TALKING TO THE GOD WHO LISTENS—Share problems they need God to listen to, then pray for partners.	Bibles

notes:

God is always ready to listen.

THE BIBLE CONNECTION

JOSHUA 1:1-9	God strengthens and encourages Joshua.
LUKE 11:1-4, 11-13	Jesus teaches that God is our heavenly Father who listens to our prayers.
LUKE 15:11-32	Jesus tells the parable of the runaway son, which portrays God as a loving parent filled with compassion.

I n this study, kids will go on a "runaway journey" to compare the experiences of real-life runaways with the feelings of isolation and loneliness they experience in their own lives.

Your group will explore the unmet needs that provoke some kids to run away. They will discover that God is willing and able to meet those needs. As a result, your kids will learn to trust the God who's always ready to listen.

Explore the verses in The Bible Connection, then examine the information in the Depthfinder boxes throughout the study to gain a deeper understanding of how these Scriptures connect with your young people.

BEFORE THE STUDY

In this study, kids will go on a "journey" in your church building or on church grounds.

Before the meeting, create the "travel routes." Make a copy of the "Runaway" handout (pp. 21-24) for every four students you expect. Post each section of each handout along a travel route. If possible, set up a different route for each group, so group members can have discussions at each stop on their journey without crowding other groups. For example, one group might make stops at the church office, the fellowship hall, the kitchen, and the gym, while another group might go to the nursery, the foyer, the parking lot, and another classroom. Be sure to note the location of the next stop at the bottom of each section of the handout.

Even if your group is restricted to your own room, kids can go on a "journey" within the room. For example, each journey group could start in a different corner of the room and move around the room in a circle. One corner of the room might be Stop 1 for one group, Stop 2 for another, and Stop 3 for a third group. To avoid confusion, copy each group's stops on a different color of paper and instruct groups to read only the directions in the colors assigned to them.

THE STUDY

FOCUSING TIME ▼

LEADER TIP

for Running Home?

If your class is larger than twenty, make two playing fields, form four teams, and have two games going at the same time.

Running Home? (5 to 10 minutes) Create a miniature baseball field in your meeting space by marking off a diamond and bases with masking tape. Form two teams to play baseball with the following rule variations (designed to give even nonathletic players a chance to make it "home"):

● The game is played with a small rubber ball.

● Players hit the ball with their hands, not with a bat.

● The pitcher is a member of the team at bat.

● All balls are counted as fair.

● To get a player out, the outfield team must tag the player, not just the base.

● Batters must run the bases clockwise.

Play as few or as many innings as time allows.

When the game is over, ask:

● **Have you ever hit a home run? How did it feel?**

● **What other sports use "home" as a goal? Why do you suppose the word "home" is used?**

Say: **Our goal in this game was to run home. Today we're going to look at what makes some young people just like you run away from home. Through our exploration today, we'll discover how God wants to help us when we feel like running away.**

LEADER TIP

for On the Run

This activity requires cooperation and leadership from the kids because they'll be moving at their own pace without adult intervention. If your kids aren't ready for this level of autonomy, consider forming larger journey groups (up to eight kids) and sending an adult with each group to help guide the experience.

RUNAWAY JOURNEY ▼

On the Run (35 to 45 minutes) Have kids form journey groups of four. Give each journey group a small notebook and a pen.

> ## DEPTHFINDER   FACTS ABOUT TEENAGE RUNAWAYS
>
> ● Although teenagers of all ages run away, the average age is fifteen.
>
> ● In most states, it's against the law for a person under eighteen to leave home. That means runaways can be picked up by the police, even if they aren't breaking any other law, and sent to juvenile homes, rehabilitation centers, or back home.
>
> ● Although statistics on runaways are largely guesswork, estimates suggest that between forty and seventy percent of teenage runaways eventually return home or are sent home.

Say: **You're going to put yourselves in the shoes of a teenage runaway. At each stop of your journey, you'll read diary entries written by real-life teenage runaways. After each reading, you'll find instructions about entries you need to make in your own "diary"—the notebook you'll carry. Have a different person read the instructions at each stop. Discuss what your entries will be, then take turns recording the entries in the diary. When you're finished, follow the directions to the next stop.**

Direct each group to its first stop.

PERSONAL APPLICATION ▼

Talking to the God Who Listens

(5 to 10 minutes)

As journey groups return, ask:

● **How did you respond to what these teenage runaways had to say?**

● **How was this experience like really running away from home?**

Say: **Most of the runaways whose comments we read seemed to feel that their parents didn't really listen to them or understand them. But <u>God is always ready to listen</u>.**

Maybe you identified with some of the frustrations the runaways mentioned. Maybe you've had to comfort a runaway. Or maybe you face different pressures or disappointments that are just as real. But you don't have to face these problems alone.

Say: **One way you can know God is with you is to read the Bible.** Ask a volunteer to read Joshua 1:1-9.

Ask:

● **Do you think Joshua was confident that God was with him? Why or why not?**

● **Do you think that knowing this changed Joshua's outlook? Why or why not?**

● **Do you think Joshua was confident that God would listen to him? Why or why not?**

LEADER TIP

for Talking to the God Who Listens

Because groups will return at different times, be prepared to repeat this activity with each group as it enters.

DEPTH FINDER — UNDERSTANDING THE BIBLE

The idea of God as a loving Father can be difficult for teenagers whose fathers are harsh or abusive. But most teenagers hope to be good parents themselves someday—think, for example, of how often teenagers say, "When I'm a parent, I'll never do that to my kids" in reference to some parental offense. Luke 11:11-13 can give even kids with lousy fathers a positive perspective of God the Father, because the passage doesn't say, "Think about your father; that's what God is like." In essence it says, "Think about the good things you would do for your children. God wants to do even more for you."

● **How is the way God talks to you different from how he talked to Joshua? How is it similar?**

● **When you feel depressed or alone, how do you know God is ready to listen to you?**

Say: **When God talked to Joshua, he said repeatedly, "Be strong and courageous" and "I will be with you." Sometimes we hear those words, and we just don't let them sink in. We might have to remind ourselves continually that God is with us. We can do that by reading the Bible, and we can do that through prayer.**

Turn to a partner and share one of the situations in which you need God to listen. Then pray for each other, remembering that <u>God is always ready to listen to you</u>. After your prayer, arrange a time to call each other this week, then pray together again about this issue over the phone.

DEPTH FINDER RUNAWAY HOT LINES

Hot line staffers offer crisis intervention and counseling, refer kids to shelters and other services, and will call parents if runaways want to let their parents know they're all right. If you or your group members know of kids who are runaways, consider calling one of these organizations:

● National Runaway Switchboard: 1-800-621-4000
● Covenant House: 1-800-999-9999

" '**M**y son,' the father said, 'you are always with me, and everything I have is yours. But we had to celebrate and be glad, because this brother of yours was dead and is alive again; he was lost and is found.' " ——**L**uke 15:31-32

Stop 1:
THE STREETS

Have someone read aloud what these real teenagers said about why they ran away. Then, as a group, discuss the entries you'll make, and have one person write them in your group diary as directed below.

Jeff, *age 15*

"I've got a couple of brothers and a couple of sisters, but I'm the oldest, and that's not the best thing. See, I get the worst part of it at home. Since I'm the oldest, they expect me to be the best. To do the most, both in school and at home. Like, I have to be an example all the others have to follow. I have to be good and get the best grades; otherwise I get hollered at.

"But I don't get all that good marks...

"And there's another thing that drove me to leaving. Once in a while my brothers and I get into a fight. See, my brothers are allowed to hit me, but if I hit them back, then I get my butt kicked by my dad. And that's not right; that's not *fair*...

"There's another reason I left, too. My dad keeps on telling me that the sooner he gets rid of me, the happier he'll be. He was real anxious to get rid of me, so I figured I'd make it easier on him and split."

Michael, *age 14*

"I guess I got into this because of school. I kinda knew I wanted to get away before this year, but it really started hard in January, after Christmas vacation. It still seems like the best idea...

"It wasn't good in past years, either. School, I mean. But it really got bad this year, the worst of all. I get pretty good marks, B's and C's—not really good, but not really bad. But there's something else, and it just got to bugging me bad. The teachers there.

"It's like the teachers' attitudes that get to me. I feel like they're always hollering at me and singling me out, picking on me. And I think the worst part of it is that I don't have any idea why. I can't explain it to myself...

"Maybe I should have told my mom what's going on in school, or told her more about it. But I didn't."

Larry, *age 16*

"It was a big problem talking with my mother. I just couldn't, you know. She couldn't *understand*. And that's another reason I left. See, I'm 16, and at that age she still wanted me to come home at nine o'clock at night. Even on Friday and Saturday night. I couldn't get over that. On weeknights I can kinda understand that I couldn't go out late, because I had homework and other things to do. But you know, like on weekends, at least to come home at eleven or a little later. Like everybody else...

"I wasn't getting into any trouble. I was good, and my mom never had any problems like that with me. So I couldn't understand why I wasn't allowed to stay out a little later. And there was no real way we could talk about it. If I brought it up, she'd just shake her head and say her way was right and that's all."

Entry 1—In your group diary, write four words that describe the emotions you think these runaways might have had.

Entry 2—Write four words that describe the emotions their statements evoke in you.

Entry 3—In as few words as possible, list the situations that these kids were running away from. (For example, "Problems with teachers.")

Entry 4—Review your list in Entry 3 and circle any of the pressures that members in your journey group can identify with.

Go to _____

Stop 2: A TEEN SHELTER

When last heard of, Larry had determined to make a complete break with his family and try to survive on his own.

Jeff and Michael, along with a girl named Annie, had been picked up by the authorities and were being sent home. Have someone read aloud these runaways' thoughts about going home. Have another person read Luke 15:11-19 aloud. Then, as a group, discuss the entries you'll make, and have one person write them in your group diary as directed below.

Jeff

"I haven't talked to my mom yet, and I guess I'm kinda scared about what's going to happen when I get home. I can't talk with my dad at all. I can talk some with my mom, but not with my dad. He gets mad real fast. Right now he's super mad. I know that. It is costing them about $25 or $30 to send me a bus ticket, and I know he's going to work that off of me. I'll be back in the house for quite a long time. I guess I'll go back because I have to, but I know I'm going to get whacked around a lot by my dad. And it ain't much fun to think of that."

Annie

"I guess I'll be glad to see my parents again. My mom and dad. Only one, I think, is supposed to come up to New York to pick me up. I guess they'll be kinda mad at this, having to make the trip and everything. But that's OK. I'll take whatever's coming. There are parts about skipping I don't really like, but there are parts I do. Right now I'd rather be home in my own room and stuff.

"But I'm glad I did *something.*"

Michael

"I sort of feel…well, I just don't know what to think. One thing I know for sure. I feel real sorry we didn't make it to Miami. Because I don't want to go back to that school, no way. It's a big problem for me, that school, like a big weight on me. And it gets worse all the time; it's all breaking up. Right now, it's like…it's like a dread of something, I guess. Like a dread of a lot of trouble that I don't know what to do with. Lots of trouble. Maybe the fact that I ran away might make a difference. I don't know. I hope so, but I don't guess much will change. I don't know how my mother is going to feel. I guess she'll be mad, but maybe she'll be glad to see me. I don't know. She's coming down to get me, and she'll get here real late. Maybe that says something. I don't know."

Entry 1—List any similarities you see between the attitudes of the modern-day runaways and the runaway son in the Bible.

Entry 2—Sketch how you imagine each runaway's face might look when meeting his or her parents for the first time after running away. Include the runaway son in the Bible passage. Label each sketch with the runaway's name.

Entry 3—List at least four ways you or people you know might try to run away from God.

Go to _____ ⟶

Home

Have someone read Luke 15:20-32 aloud. Then, as a group, discuss the entries you'll make, and have one person write them in your group diary as directed below.

Entry 1—List three words that describe how the runaway son might have felt when his father welcomed him home.

Entry 2—Based on the character of the father in Luke 15:11-32, create a list of the qualities of the "ideal parent"—the kind of parent who runaways would want to return home to.

Entry 3—For each person in your journey group, write a word or phrase that describes how that person feels having God as a parent they can always "come home" to.

Go to _____ →

Home

Have someone read Luke 11:1-4, 11-13 aloud. Then, as a group, discuss the entries you'll make, and have one person write them in your group diary as directed below.

Entry 1—Most of the runaways whose comments we read seemed to feel that their parents didn't really listen to them or understand them. But God is always ready to listen. List at least three current situations in which you need God to listen.

Entry 2—Look back at the qualities of the ideal parent you listed at the last stop. Have each person in your journey group share which quality is most meaningful to him or her, and why. Then pray together, thanking or praising God for having those qualities.

Entry 3—If God is our Father, that makes us a family. List the people in your journey group. After each name, write one reason you're glad to be in the same "family" as that person. (For example, "I'm glad to have a 'sister' who is as cheerful as Karen.")

← Return to your original meeting room.

When God Seems Silent

"I prayed... nothing happened."

God

by **M**ike **N**appa

■ "I prayed...nothing happened." ■ How many times have you heard that lament from your young people? ■ And yet, even after weeks or months of seeking God, when the apparent "silence of heaven" pushes them to feel angry and confused, they still won't stop. They keep praying—hoping God will hear them, hoping he will answer, and hoping they might stumble upon the secret to this mysterious link with God we call prayer. ■ When we asked real-life teenagers on America Online to share their thoughts on prayer, the response was overwhelming. This study focuses on those teenagers' honest comments—to help your group members expose their own doubts about prayer and discover the truth that they serve a God who always hears their cries and always answers.

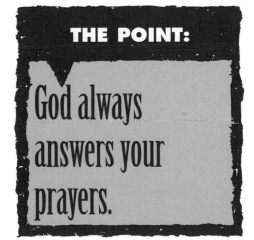

THE POINT:

God always answers your prayers.

The Study
AT A GLANCE

SECTION	MINUTES	WHAT STUDENTS WILL DO	SUPPLIES
Starting Out	5 to 10	PRAYER COVERING—Commit to praying for the class in five-minute intervals.	Paper, pencil
Exploration 1	15 to 20	VIEWS OF PRAYER—Debate several opinions on the topic of prayer.	"Views of Prayer" handout (p. 33), scissors, tape
Exploration 2	10 to 15	UNANSWERED PRAYER?—Look for the emotion behind two prayers in Scripture and discuss their questions about those Scriptures.	Bibles
	up to 10	QUESTIONS ON PRAYER—Ask questions about prayer for other groups to answer as though they were Jesus or Paul.	Bibles, index cards, pencils
Wrapping Up	5 to 10	PRAYER CHALLENGE CAMPAIGN—Organize a weeklong campaign of prayer.	Paper, pencils, calendar

notes:

God always answers your prayers.

THE BIBLE CONNECTION

MATTHEW 26:36-46   Jesus prays that God would remove from him the impending "cup of suffering," Jesus' death on the cross.

2 CORINTHIANS 12:7-10   Paul reports that he prayed three times for God to remove a "thorn" from his flesh, and three times God refused.

I n this study, kids will examine several views of prayer and will ask questions about two experiences of seemingly "unanswered prayer" recorded in the Bible. Then they'll compare those views and scriptural experiences to their own experiences with prayer.

By doing this, kids will discover their misconceptions about prayer and be challenged to pursue an intimate prayer relationship with an infinite, caring God.

Explore the verses in The Bible Connection, then study the information in the Depthfinder boxes throughout the study to gain a deeper understanding of how these Scriptures connect with your young people.

BEFORE THE STUDY

Before class, designate an area near your meeting room (or in an out-of-the-way corner of your meeting room) as a "praying spot." Next, list on a sheet of paper the time your group meets (broken into five-minute intervals), following each entry with a blank line for writing a person's name. For example, you might write

7:00 _____
7:05 _____
7:10 _____

and so on, until you've broken up your entire class time into five-minute blocks.

Also, photocopy and cut apart the quotes in the "Views of Prayer" handout (p. 33). Tape the quotes on walls all over your meeting room. (It's OK to post the same quote in more than one place.)

LEADER TIP for The Study

Whenever groups are discussing several questions, write the questions on newsprint and tape it to the wall. That way, kids can move through the discussion at their own pace.

LEADER TIP for The Study

Don't forget to quietly check every once in a while to make sure that at least one person is at the praying spot described in the "Prayer Covering" activity at all times during the class session.

LEADER TIP
for The Study

At times, group discussion can take longer than you may have planned. You might not have time for teenagers to discuss all the questions in this study—that's OK. If time's running short, simply choose and focus on the two or three questions from an activity that you feel would best meet your teenagers' needs.

THE STUDY

STARTING OUT ▼

Prayer Covering (5 to 10 minutes)

As kids arrive, ask for volunteers willing to help "cover" your time together in prayer by spending five minutes during class talking to God in the praying spot. If necessary to fill up the class time, allow students to sign up for more than one five-minute time block. You might also consider allowing more than one student to sign up for the same time block.

Instruct all volunteers to keep an eye on the clock and to quietly excuse themselves from whatever's happening to go and pray at the appropriate times.

For some teenagers, praying for five minutes might seem like an eternity. To help kids pray in a more directed way, you might want to offer them suggestions from the "Things to Pray About" box below. (Feel free to photocopy that box and place it at the praying spot.)

LEADER TIP
for Exploration 1

If all students gather on one side in response to a quote, ask for a few volunteers to play the "devil's advocate" and defend the opposite viewpoint.

EXPLORATION 1

Views of Prayer (15 to 20 minutes)

Have kids form a circle in the middle of the room. Tell everyone to face away from the center of the circle. Then say: **Today we're going to examine the idea of prayer, and I'd like to hear your views about this topic. Posted all around the room are**

THINGS TO PRAY ABOUT

● Think of all the descriptive words about God, then pray, "God, you are..." and complete the sentence with the words you thought of.

● Think of three things you did (or didn't do!) over the past seven days that you know God wouldn't approve of. Then describe those things to God and ask him to forgive those past mistakes.

● Think of five good things about your life. Then thank God for those things.

● Pray for each person in your class by name, asking that God would show kindness and love to that person in some tangible way.

● Ask God to guide your youth group leader during this meeting so you can all have a great time of discovery together.

quotes expressing a variety of perspectives on prayer. You've got three minutes to examine the quotes and carry back to this circle the quote that most expresses the way you feel about prayer. Ready? Go.

After everyone has chosen a quote, have kids gather near you and toss their chosen quotes into a pile. One by one, select a quote from the pile, read it aloud, then say: **If you agree with this quote, move to my left. If you disagree, move to my right.**

Wait for kids to respond, then ask a few people from each group to defend their choices.

Read as many quotes as time allows. Then have everyone find a partner and sit down to discuss these questions:

● **Why do you think there are so many different opinions about prayer?**

● **Have you ever felt that prayer might be a waste of time? Explain.**

● **Why do you suppose virtually all major religions teach about prayer or something similar, such as meditation?**

● **When has prayer made a difference in your life?**

● **What's one question you have about prayer? How do you think you might find an answer to that question?**

● **Why do you think some prayers seem to go unanswered?**

Ask a few pairs to report the results of their discussions to the rest of the class. Then say: **I believe <u>God always answers your prayers</u>, but I also know that even the Bible tells of times when it seemed that God refused to respond to a prayer. Let's look into this more.**

EXPLORATION 2

Unanswered Prayer? (10 to 15 minutes)
Have kids form foursomes, then assign each group these two passages: Matthew 26:36-46 and 2 Corinthians 12:7-10. Tell kids not to read their passages yet.

Say: **In a moment, we're going to read about two people in the Bible whose prayers seemed to go unanswered. But to make this reading a bit challenging, let's try reading the passages from a distance.**

DEPTHFINDER   UNDERSTANDING THE BIBLE

In 2 Corinthians 12:7-10, Paul refers to a "thorn in [his] flesh." Scholars disagree about what that "thorn" might have been. Some say it was simply temptation. Others think it might have been things such as opposition to his faith, bad vision, headaches, epilepsy, malaria, or a speech impediment. But regardless of what the problem was, it's important to note that God did answer Paul's prayer. Paul wanted healing; God's answer was grace in weakness instead.

Have each group open a Bible to Matthew 26:36-46, prop the open Bible against a wall, then step back about seven or eight feet. Tell groups to work as a team to read the passage from that distance—without stepping forward. (If kids need to turn a page to read the whole passage, have them select a "designated flipper" to move forward, flip the page, then return to the group.)

Repeat this process for both passages. When groups finish, have them collect their Bibles to see how accurately they were able to read the passage. Then have foursomes discuss these questions:

● **How did trying to read the passages from a distance make you feel?**

● **How is that like trying to pray when God seems silent or far away?**

● **What do you do when God seems silent?**

Ask volunteers to read aloud each of the passages again for the whole group. Then have foursomes continue their discussions with these questions:

● **What are your thoughts about prayer after hearing about the experiences of Jesus and Paul in these two passages?**

● **How were Jesus and Paul able to remain strong in their faith despite these seemingly unanswered prayers?**

● **Do you think Jesus or Paul would agree with the statement "God always answers your prayers"? Why or why not?**

● **What would it take for you to believe that God always answers your prayers? Explain.**

Questions on Prayer (up to 10 minutes)

Have teenagers assign the following roles within their groups: a Company Clerk, who records the group's thoughts on an index card; a Squad Leader, who coordinates the group discussion; a Field Reporter, who'll report the group's answers to the class; and a Morale Officer, who watches to make sure everyone participates in the discussion.

Give an index card and a pencil to each Company Clerk. Say: **You've read about these prayer experiences of Jesus and Paul. Now let's imagine that you could ask Jesus or Paul any question at all about your experiences with prayer. What's the one question your group would ask?**

Give groups two minutes to discuss their ideas. When all groups have a question written on their cards, have foursomes trade cards with each other. Then give groups about three minutes to answer the questions as if they were Jesus or Paul.

When everyone's ready, have groups take turns reading the questions and sharing their answers with the class. Have as many groups share as time allows. Then gather everyone in a circle once more, this time facing inward. Ask:

● **If you believe that <u>God always answers your prayers</u>, how will that affect your attitudes and actions this week?**

Say: **<u>God always answers your prayers</u>, but prayers don't always have to be requests. In fact, I'd like us to take a minute right now to say a prayer of thanks to God.**

Think for a moment about one or two words that describe a positive contribution the person on your right has made to our meeting time today. For example, you might choose "enthusiasm" because the person to your right participated enthusiastically. Or you might choose "insightful" because that person put a lot of thought into his or her answers during our discussions.

Pause while students think of appropriate words. Then say: **I'm going to begin a sentence to start our prayer. Then I'd like us to go around the circle and take turns saying our chosen words as the way to complete the sentence and the prayer.**

When everyone's ready, pray: **Lord, thank you so much for using the people in this circle to contribute the following things to this class...** Add a positive word or two about the person to your right. After everyone has had a turn, close the prayer by saying: **Amen.**

LEADER TIP
for Questions on Prayer

If some groups struggle with trying to figure out how Jesus or Paul might respond to their questions, encourage them to look up additional Scriptures that describe these men's characters in more detail. Here are some examples:
● Jesus—Matthew 6:5-15, 25-34 and 7:7-11.
● Paul—Romans 8:26-28; Ephesians 6:18-20; Philippians 4:6-7; and 1 Thessalonians 5:16-18.

DEPTHFINDER — UNDERSTANDING THESE KIDS

Many teenagers today—and likely some teenagers in your youth group—distrust the idea that praying to an invisible God can actually impact their lives. In fact, two-thirds of the people described as Generation X-ers say they believe that "If you don't look out for your own best interests, you can be sure no one else will either."

Christian researcher George Barna describes today's generation of young people this way: "They feel estranged from God, separated from each other, lacking meaning in life, void of roots and societal connection. In short, they feel alienated from life."

The message for this generation is simple: There's a God who will look out for your best interests, who will enter into an intimate relationship with you, and who will answer your prayers.

Prayer Challenge Campaign

(5 to 10 minutes)

Say: **We've raised a lot of questions about prayer today, but the most basic question we have to ask is this: Does <u>God always answer prayer</u>? I propose we do a little experiment to find out.**

Encourage kids to organize a Prayer Challenge Campaign. Tell them the campaign's goal is simply to get as many people as they can to commit to praying the following prayer at least once a day for seven days: "Lord, show me this week whether or not prayer is worthwhile."

Spend the rest of your class time planning the campaign's details. Have kids designate a week within the next month as the prayer week. Then take as much time as you have to plan strategies for encouraging people to sign up for the campaign. For example, kids might make fliers and take them to school, take out an ad in the school or local newspaper, or simply ask ten people to try it.

Set a date for a follow-up meeting to debrief the experience after the week of prayer. Invite everyone who participated to come and report the results of their prayer experiments. Use that meeting to help kids discover how God might have answered their prayers and to examine why or why not prayers may seem to have gone unanswered for some.

❝Three times I pleaded with the Lord to take it away from me. But he said to me, ʻMy grace is sufficient for you, for my power is made perfect in weakness.ʼ Therefore I will boast all the more gladly about my weaknesses, so that Christ's power may rest on me.**❞**

—2 Corinthians 12:8-9

Views of Prayer

Photocopy and cut apart the quotes on this page for use in the "Views of Prayer" activity.

"Any thoughts on prayer?
    Yeah. It's dumb."

—Phlanax, from America Online

- -

"Prayer is a very powerful thing…it works for me."

—Bridget2, from America Online

- -

"Prayer = brownie points with God."

—Dave 911, from America Online

- -

"I believe in God, but I don't think God answers every prayer.
    One in 10,000 maybe."

—Brenke, from America Online

- -

"So [you must] think clearly and control yourselves so you will be able to pray."

—Peter, from the Bible (I Peter 4:7b)

- -

"I'm curious what makes people [pray]. It seems pointless to me."

—Cuillin 2, from America Online

- -

"I think whether [prayer] works or not depends on the person praying. If you think it works,
    it probably will."

—JENNYN3010, from America Online

- -

"Anyone who is having troubles should pray…When a believing person prays, great things happen."

—James, from the Bible (James 5:13a and 16b, New Century Version)

- -

"I don't think God really cares what God you pray to as long as you've said your prayers."

—KathG, from America Online

 **We Trust**

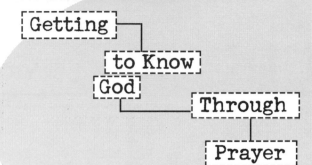

Getting to Know God Through Prayer

by Debbie Gowensmith

THE POINT:

Prayer builds a trusting relationship.

■ Amy listens to music that reminds her of God. ■ Michael writes about his fears and hopes in a journal. ■ Kelly sings praise songs as she cleans her room. ■ Michelle thinks about God's majesty as she hikes. ■ Scott paints with bright colors that make him think of God's glory. ■ Sara kneels beside her bed with her hands clasped. ■ In their own ways, they are praying. They're reaching up to God in personally meaningful ways. Through their own words—or through no words at all—they are aware of an intimate, exciting, growing connection with God. ■ This kind of connection builds our trust in God. As we share more and more of our lives with him, we learn to trust him more and more. As we spend more time sharing ourselves with him, our faith in him develops. The relationship grows stronger and stronger. ■ Are your kids building that kind of connection? Or do they think prayer is meaningless, boring, or confusing? Because only forty-two percent of teenagers say they pray frequently (George H. Gallup International Institute, *The Religious Life of Young Americans*), you want to make sure your kids understand prayer. You can help them become closer to their Father by teaching them that prayer can be trusting, personal, and even fun. Through this study, your kids can develop a prayer life that builds their trust in God.

The Study
AT A GLANCE

SECTION	MINUTES	WHAT STUDENTS WILL DO	SUPPLIES
Object Opener	10 to 15	TRUST ME—Hold objects—first without and then with communication—while blindfolded.	Bibles, blindfolds, jigsaw puzzle pieces
Biblical Exploration	20 to 25	THE WHOLE PICTURE—Try to decipher a picture using only a few puzzle pieces, then "report" the story of Hannah.	Bibles, jigsaw puzzle pieces, paper, pens or pencils
Personal Prayer	10 to 15	PRAY MY WAY—Say the Lord's Prayer, first with rules and then without rules.	Bibles, "Prayer Rules" handouts (p. 44), pens or pencils
Closing Celebration	5 to 10	IT'S A PRAYER PARTY—Explore fun ways to pray.	Bibles, various supplies as explained in the "Before the Study" box (p. 37)

notes:

Prayer builds a trusting relationship.

THE BIBLE CONNECTION

1 SAMUEL 1:1-20, 24-28; 2:1-11	Hannah shares both her most painful experiences and her most joyous experiences with God through prayer.
PROVERBS 3:5-6	Solomon recognizes the wisdom of trusting God completely.
MATTHEW 6:9-13	Jesus teaches the people a new way to pray.
1 THESSALONIANS 5:16-18	Paul encourages joyful, continual prayer.

I n this study, kids will explore trust and communication by holding different objects while blindfolded, will re-create the story of Hannah, will pray with and without strict rules, and will celebrate prayer by exploring fun ways to pray.

Through these experiences, kids can learn that a trusting relationship with God can best develop through prayer that is fulfilling, personal, and even fun.

Explore the verses in The Bible Connection, then examine the information in the Depthfinder boxes throughout the study to gain a deeper understanding of how these Scriptures connect with your young people.

BEFORE THE STUDY

For "Pray My Way," make a photocopy of the "Prayer Rules" handout (p. 44) for every two people in your class. (Kids will work on this handout in pairs.)

For "It's a Prayer Party," collect as many supplies as you can think of that kids could use to pray creatively. The idea is to allow kids to explore prayer through different learning styles, hobbies, and interests. For example, you might provide a Polaroid camera, a tape recorder and blank audiocassette, music, markers, crayons, paper, scissors, string, bubble solution and wands, small musical instruments, floor pillows, a globe, a newspaper, and a calendar.

LEADER TIP for The Study

Whenever groups discuss a list of questions, write the questions on newsprint and tape the newsprint to the wall so groups can discuss the questions at their own pace.

THE STUDY

OBJECT OPENER ▼

LEADER TIP
for Trust Me

As you move along the line with the puzzle pieces, don't push people who say they aren't ready. Instead, say: **That's OK. I'll just go to the next person.** Then during the discussion, incorporate the following questions:

● What was your reaction when I respected your feelings and didn't hand you anything?

● How was that like or unlike a trusting relationship?

Trust Me (10 to 15 minutes)
After everyone has arrived, say a short prayer asking God to make this group's time together informative and inspiring. Then have kids line up shoulder to shoulder. Give each person a blindfold, and ask kids to put the blindfolds on. Then say: **Put your hands out in front of you because I'm going to hand you something.** Don't tell the kids what you're going to hand them; just walk silently down the line and place a Bible in each person's hands.

After you've given everyone a Bible, tell kids they may temporarily remove their blindfolds. Ask:

● **How did it feel to be blindfolded and to hold out your hands for an unknown object? Why?**

● **If you felt unsure, why did you hold out your hands anyway?**

● **How was holding out your hands like or unlike trusting someone?**

Have everyone look up Proverbs 3:5-6, and ask a volunteer to read the verses aloud. Then ask:

● **What does this Scripture say about trusting God?**

● **Is it easy or difficult to trust God with all your heart? Why?**

● **In a relationship with a friend, how can trust grow?**

● **In your relationship with God, how can trust grow?**

Have kids put on their blindfolds again. Then say: **Now I'm going**

DEPTH FINDER — TEACHING KIDS TO PRAY

Because prayer nurtures kids' relationship with God, it is essential. So how do you help your kids learn how to pray? "Because [prayer] is profoundly relational, what you are trying to teach is not so much mechanics as how to nurture and develop a relationship," says Walt Marcum, an ordained pastor and youth minister. He suggests several guidelines for teaching kids to pray, including the following:

● "Model prayer."
● "Practice prayer."
● "Provide opportunities to pray."
● "Use techniques that involve everyone."
● "Communicate expectations."
● "Allow [kids] to determine the content of their own prayers."
● "Provide an environment of prayer."
● "Allow time for prayer to develop."

(Source: Walt Marcum, "Prayer: Speaking to God," Leader, June/July/August 1995.)

to hand you something else. **It's not harmful or disgusting. You'll feel small, very lightweight pieces of something.** Walk along the line again, but before you place a couple of jigsaw puzzle pieces in each person's hands, ask: [Name of person], **are you ready? Are you sure? Do you trust me? OK, I'm starting.**

After you've distributed the puzzle pieces, tell kids to take off their blindfolds. Have kids set aside their puzzle pieces to use later, and ask:

● **Because I handed you Bibles last time, did you feel better about what I might hand you this time? Explain.**

● **Based on your experience in this activity, how do you think communication affects trust?**

● **How does communication with God affect trust?**

Say: **For trust to develop with anyone, it requires communication. Because we communicate with God through prayer, <u>prayer builds a trusting relationship with God</u>.**  Let's explore that idea further.

BIBLICAL EXPLORATION ▼

The Whole Picture (20 to 25 minutes) With their puzzle pieces from the previous activity in hand, have kids form groups of four. Say: **We've talked about how communication enhances trust in a relationship. Now let's see what kind of communication helps to build trust.** Tell kids to talk within their foursomes about their puzzle pieces to figure out what the whole puzzle picture is.

After about a minute, call time. Then have kids discuss these questions in their foursomes:

● **Was it easy or difficult to figure out the whole picture based on your puzzle pieces? Why?**

● **How is that like sharing only a few pieces of your life with someone?**

● **How is the trust in a relationship affected when one person shares only a few pieces of his or her life with the other person?**

● **What would your relationship with God be like if you shared with him only one piece of your life? all the pieces of your life?**

Say: **We may be tempted to share with God only pieces of ourselves. <u>Prayer builds a trusting relationship</u> when you share everything with God—your entire life, not just certain elements of your life. Let's look in the Bible for an example of someone who shared with God all the elements of her life.**

Have kids form seven groups. Assign the groups Scripture passages as indicated below and on the following page:

● Group 1—1 Samuel 1:1-8
● Group 2—1 Samuel 1:9-14
● Group 3—1 Samuel 1:15-18
● Group 4—1 Samuel 1:19-20, 24-28
● Group 5—1 Samuel 2:1-2
● Group 6—1 Samuel 2:3-8

LEADER TIP for The Whole Picture

If kids complain that they can't possibly figure out the whole picture based on their puzzle pieces, just encourage them to keep trying and to talk with their group members. If some kids do figure out the whole picture, ask them during the debriefing how communication helped them to solve the puzzle.

LEADER TIP

for The Whole Picture

Ideally, each group in this activity should have *at least* three students. If you have fewer than twenty-one students, have one group use the Scriptures listed for Groups 2 and 3, and another group use the Scriptures listed for Groups 5 and 6. If you have only six kids, have one student use the Scriptures listed for Groups 2 and 3.

● Group 7—1 Samuel 2:9-11

Tell groups they have about ten minutes to prepare a "live news report" of their Scripture passages. In these reports, all the kids must play roles: news anchors or "on-the-scene" reporters and characters.

After several minutes, ask Group 1 to present its report to the class; after that, ask Group 2 and then Group 3 to present their reports. Applaud each group's presentation. Then ask:

● **What has Hannah felt so far in this story?**

● **Do you think Hannah trusted God? Why or why not?**

● **How did your understanding of the story change as you watched each group's presentation?**

● **How is that like sharing everything with God through prayer?**

Distribute a sheet of paper and a pen or pencil to each person. Say: **Just as Hannah talked to God about her painful experience, take a minute to write a short prayer to God about something that's bothering or hurting you.**

After about a minute, ask Groups 4, 5, 6, and 7 to share their news reports. Again, applaud each group after its presentation. Then ask:

● **In this part of the story, how did Hannah feel?**

● **Why do you think Hannah shared both her painful times and her joyous times with God?**

● **Again, how did your understanding of the story change as you heard more about it?**

● **How is that like sharing everything with God through prayer?**

Say: **Just as Hannah talked to God about her joy, take a minute to write a short prayer to God about something you're thankful for.** After about a minute, say: **In this activity, your understanding of Hannah's story changed as the story became more complete.**

DEPTHFINDER — UNDERSTANDING TRUSTING RELATIONSHIPS

Intimate relationships—the supportive, accepting relationships most people desire—are built through the development of caring, sharing, trust, commitment, honesty, empathy, and tenderness (William H. Masters, et al., *Human Sexuality*).

As part of those elite characteristics, trust proves itself vital not only to healthy human relationships, but also to a healthy, growing relationship with God. And trust requires the other elements, such as commitment and honesty, because trust doesn't usually happen immediately. It develops over time through honest, caring communication.

The process begins when you share a little bit of your life with God. Through sharing, you learn that God is a caring, tender Father who loves you. So you share a little more. Over time, you learn that God has your best interests at heart, which encourages you to share even more. As you continue to share openly and honestly, the relationship strengthens. You discover your trust in God grows and strengthens continually. You discover that this process never ends; God's love for you is everlasting.

You also learned about a person who shared a complete picture of her life with God through prayer. And you wrote prayers expressing to God both a struggle and a joy in your life. Ask:

● **Based on these experiences, do you think sharing everything with God can build trust in your relationship with God? Why or why not?**

● **Because God knows everything, do you think it's important for us to share everything with God? Why or why not?** (You may want to use the "Telling God Everything" Depthfinder on page 43 to encourage further discussion about this important question.)

Say: **The more we share about ourselves in a relationship, the more we learn to trust the person we're sharing with. Prayer builds a trusting relationship with God, especially when we tell him about all parts of our lives. But how do we tell God about our lives? We'll look at that next.**

PERSONAL PRAYER ▼

Pray My Way (10 to 15 minutes)
Have everyone find a partner, then give each pair a "Prayer Rules" handout (p. 44) and a pen or pencil. Give kids about five minutes to complete their handouts.

Then have kids discuss the following questions with their partners:

● **What was it like to pray using someone else's words and rules?**

● **When you had the chance to change the prayer, did you pray the original way? Why or why not?**

● **Did the prayer become more meaningful when you got to pray your own way?**

● **How do you think praying in a personal way can help build trust in God?**

Say: **In the Gospels, Jesus gives us themes to use when we pray to God and shows us how personal prayer builds a trusting relationship. When we share ourselves with someone, we can learn to trust that person. When we talk to God from our own hearts about our own lives, we share our true selves with him. Let's try that now.**

CLOSING CELEBRATION ▼

It's a Prayer Party (5 to 10 minutes)
On a table, set out all the supplies you gathered before the study. Say: **Today you've experienced firsthand how communication helps to build trust. You've studied a woman who shared her life with God through prayer to learn that the more you share, the more you learn to trust someone. You've experienced that when you pray personally, with words and actions**

you relate to, <u>**prayer builds a trusting relationship.**</u> Ask:
- **How do you spend time with your friends?**
- **How does sharing experiences build trust in your relationships?**
- **Do you think you can share your life with God in the same ways? Why or why not?**

Have kids open their Bibles to 1 Thessalonians 5:16-18, and ask a volunteer to read the passage aloud. Then have kids discuss these questions with partners:
- **What kinds of things would you do to "be joyful always"?**
- **If God likes us to be joyful always, pray continually, and give thanks in all circumstances, how do you think that should affect your prayer life?**
- **Do you think fun builds trust in a relationship? Why or why not?**
- **How do you think you could incorporate fun into your prayer life?**

Say: **We like to share our hobbies and interests with our friends. Fun is one of the best things people can share in a relationship. Fun can build trust because when we're having fun together, we relax and build new experiences with each other. We're also motivated to spend time with each other if we have fun together.**

DEPTHFINDER

DID HANNAH TRY TO "BRIBE" GOD?

When kids read the story of Hannah, they may question her methods. On the surface, Hannah seemed to approach God with a lack of respect and a brash request: "Give me a son, and he'll be a man of God."

Looking deeper, though, reveals a different scene. "There is no demanding or threatening here. Her prayer is not formal, contrived or ritualistic. It is as direct as any might wish it to be...God was not obligated to answer her. But the fact that he did indicates that he judged her motives to be right and her request appropriate" (Walter C. Kaiser Jr., et al., *Hard Sayings of the Bible*).

Hannah trusted God completely. She knew that only he could affect her barrenness. Far from revealing disrespect, her prayer reveals her deeply personal relationship, her humility, and her dependence on God.

If your kids see Hannah's prayer as evidence that God can be bargained with, help them understand what true prayer is. "Prayer is not a means of compelling greater powers to do our bidding...Prayer is communication between persons, involving all the variables of personal wishes, commitments, integrity, understanding, and will...Assurance [that requests have been answered] arises, not from the manipulation of circumstances, but from *knowing* the persons involved. Those who best know an individual know whether their request to him was answered by coincidence or because they asked. Those who best know the God of the Bible can assess the efficacy of prayer as request to Him...Prayer ought never to be turned into magical compulsion, but must always remain request to a wiser, personal God" (The Zondervan Pictorial Encyclopedia of the Bible).

DEPTH FINDER — TELLING GOD EVERYTHING

God knows what we need before we even ask (Matthew 6:8), so why should we tell God about all the pieces of our lives?

Some kids may be surprised to learn that prayer is not just for God; it's for us. "Prayer is a tool God has given us for our own benefit...It is talking to God and listening to God. Prayer makes us aware of who we are, of who God is, of what we need, and from whom we get what we need. Through prayer—in all of its many forms—we enter into communion and conversation with God" (Walt Marcum, "Prayer: Speaking to God," Leader, June/July/August 1995).

Through this conversation, our relationship with God builds. We learn how much we need him and how much he cares for us. We see his wisdom and grace in our lives when we stay connected with him.

The more we share with God, the more we open our hearts to his influence. "Prayer can change us rather than the situation, reinforcing our confidence in our God's sufficiency and realigning our will with his will" (The Quest Study Bible). Instead of closing him off from pieces of ourselves, praying to God about everything ensures that we'll hear his voice in every area of our lives. "God wants us to give him *everything*—school, work, sports, activities, family, and so on," says high school student Bonnie Richard ("Why Pray?" Campus Life, July/August 1997). After all, she adds, "He can do what we can't. *That's* why we pray."

Point out all of the supplies displayed on the table. Tell kids they have the rest of the class time to pray to God in a very personal and fun way. Encourage kids to explore different ways to pray. For example, they could take photographs of things that remind them of God's goodness, play music, write poetry, draw pictures, use a globe or map to think about people throughout the world, hug friends, or sit and think about who God is or what he's done for us.

To close, say: **Today you've learned how <u>prayer builds a trusting relationship</u>. You've also experienced several different types of prayer: I opened with a group prayer, you wrote down prayers, you prayed with partners, and you experimented with active prayer. To close, let's share a silent group prayer. I'll start us out, and then we can all pray silently.** Pray: **Lord, thank you for giving us prayer, through which we can communicate with you. Continue to show us how to build our trust in you through prayer. Now please hear us as we pray silently about our week.**

After a minute of silent prayer, close by saying: **In Jesus' name, amen.**

Prayer **RULES**

With your partner, read Matthew 6:9-13 while following these rules:

1. You must kneel on both knees.

2. You must place your palms together.

3. You must hold your hands up directly in front of your nose.

4. You must keep your Bible open on the floor in front of you.

5. You must keep your eyes open.

6. You must read the prayer aloud—but in a whisper only you and your partner can hear.

7. You must alternate verses. For example, one partner must read verses 9, 11, and 13, and the other partner must read verses 10 and 12.

With your partner, pray the **Lord's Prayer** again. This time, though, make it personal. You can use or lose the rules above. Sit or stand, close your eyes or keep them open, whisper the prayer or sing it. You can even use the space below to write different words for the prayer—words that better fit your life.

Will Power:
Finding · a · Way · to · Focus · on · God

BY MIKAL KEEFER

■ It may not seem like a topic you need to discuss with your kids. In the Big-Mac-and-fries world we live in, they might think fasting is a thing of the past. They may think fasting is simply about Jewish tradition. Their church may already have defined guidelines on how and when to fast. ■ What kids need to know is that fasting isn't about tradition, doctrine, or law. It's about focusing on God. ■ Intellectually, it can clear our minds. ■ Spiritually, it can help us focus and listen. ■ Fasting is one means of concentrated spiritual discipline. ■ It's not about food. It's not about hunger. ■ Fasting is about prayer. ■ Talking to your kids about fasting will help them identify their misconceptions and realize that their communication with God is what's important. Teach them how to focus, how to listen, and how to make fasting—or any other form of prayer—a spiritually strengthening experience.

THE POINT:

We need to focus on God.

The Study
AT A GLANCE

SECTION	MINUTES	WHAT STUDENTS WILL DO	SUPPLIES
Introduction	up to 10	INSTANT INTIMACY—Write letters and discuss how to build a relationship with God.	Cassette or CD of soothing music, cassette or CD player, pencils, paper
Bible Exploration	10 to 15	STAYING FOCUSED—Practice focusing while they pray.	Bibles, ice cubes, paper towels, "Fast Fasting Facts" handouts (p. 55)
Life Application	10 to 15	FASTING FOR FUN AND PROFIT—Examine Bible passages so they can give advice about profitable fasting to a proud Pharisee.	Bibles
	10 to 15	CROSS SEARCH—Find crosses on a quick field trip, then discuss "prayer triggers" to place in their lives.	Bible, watches, paper, pencils, chalkboard and chalk or newsprint and marker
Closing	5 to 10	OUR FATHER—Share in a directed prayer.	Cassette or CD of soothing music, cassette or CD player, watch

notes:

We need to focus on God.

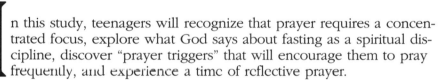

THE BIBLE CONNECTION

ISAIAH 1:13-14; 58:6-7; and MATTHEW 6:16-18	These verses explain that offerings to God, such as fasting, should be meaningful and should reflect our service and humility.
MATTHEW 6:9b-13	Jesus gives us the Lord's Prayer as an example of how we should pray.
EPHESIANS 6:18	Paul tells us to be prepared to pray at all times.
JOSHUA 7:2-7; 2 SAMUEL 12:13-20; NEHEMIAH 1:1-4; DANIEL 10:1-3; and MATTHEW 4:1-2	These verses describe the various purposes that fasting served in biblical times.

I n this study, teenagers will recognize that prayer requires a concentrated focus, explore what God says about fasting as a spiritual discipline, discover "prayer triggers" that will encourage them to pray frequently, and experience a time of reflective prayer.

By doing this, teenagers will see the value of regular and meaningful prayer and will take practical steps to incorporate focused prayer in their lives.

Explore the verses in The Bible Connection, then examine the information in the Depthfinder boxes throughout the study to gain a deeper understanding of how these Scriptures connect with your young people.

BEFORE THE STUDY

Make one photocopy of the "Fast Fasting Facts" handout (p. 55) for each student.

LEADER TIP for The Study

Whenever groups discuss a list of questions, write the questions on newsprint and tape the newsprint to the wall so groups can discuss the questions at their own pace.

THE STUDY

INTRODUCTION ▼

LEADER TIP

for Instant Intimacy

Play simple, instrumental music so students don't listen to lyrics instead of concentrating. You might choose music by Phil Keaggy, Eric Tingstad, or Enya.

Instant Intimacy (up to 10 minutes)
As you play gentle, soothing music in the background, distribute pencils and paper to students. Say: **Move around and find a comfortable place where you can relax and write easily. Settle in so you can write a letter to a friend—someone you haven't seen for a while but with whom you want to stay in touch.**

Then say: **Ready? Great. You have precisely 7.5 seconds to write your letter to your old friend.** While kids are writing, recite the following prayer out loud:

"Dear God, thank you for this food and the hands that prepared it. Bless it to our bodies and us to your service. Amen."

Say: **OK, time's up! That's a standard pre-lunch prayer, delivered quickly, with head bowed and eyes closed and containing exactly no thought or feeling.**

Ask teenagers to form pairs. Say: **Let's compare that prayer with the letter you were preparing to write to your friend.**

Have students discuss these questions:

● **What did you write about in your letter to an old friend?**

● **What did you decide, in the short time you had to write, to say to your friend?**

● **Was it the most important thing you had to say? Why or why not?**

● **If you had just 7.5 seconds to say something important to God, what would it be?**

Ask volunteers to share what they decided during their discussions.

Say: **When we pray, we're building a relationship with God. Thoughtless routines and words said out of habit don't build a relationship. That's true with our friends, and that's true with God. That's why <u>we need to focus on God</u>.**
Whether we're praying for 7.5 seconds or 7.5 hours, the

DEPTH FINDER UNDERSTANDING THE BIBLE

Jesus' teachings were first heard by a culture familiar with fasting. Throughout all periods of Israelite history, fasts were proclaimed as a response to national emergencies (Judges 20:26; 1 Samuel 7:6), as an act of penitence (1 Kings 21:27; Nehemiah 9:1), in conjunction with heartfelt private or public prayer (2 Samuel 12:16; Luke 2:36-38), or as part of mourning (2 Samuel 1:12). And each of these motivations for fasting remains valid today.

goal is to open our hearts and minds to honestly come before our heavenly Father.

Since you're comfortable, let's write that letter to an old friend—God. Nobody else will read it. Take a few minutes to tell God what you're thinking these days, what you're feeling, what you're facing. You've got about five minutes.

Give two- and one-minute countdown warnings. Ask kids to gather again and to place their letters in a private, out-of-sight place such as their pockets.

BIBLE EXPLORATION ▼

Staying Focused (10 to 15 minutes)

Ask teenagers to form pairs. Distribute one ice cube to each teenager. Say: **I'd like you to hold this ice cube in your right hand as you discuss the following questions. Please do not put your ice cube down or move it from your hand.**

Say:

● **Think of one adult who seemed to really listen to you when you were a child. Tell about a time you felt listened to by this adult.**

● **How important is it to listen to others when you're talking with them? Why?**

● **How can you tell if someone is listening to you? How do you let others know you're listening?**

As teenagers talk, the cold, melting ice will cause them to become increasingly uncomfortable, and they will have trouble focusing on the discussion. Before the students put their ice cubes down, ask:

● **Has it been easy to listen to your partner as you held an ice cube? Why or why not?**

Collect ice cubes, and hand out paper towels so teenagers can dry their hands and clean up any melted water on the floor. Say: **If prayer is communication with God, both speaking and listening are involved. In your newly de-iced pairs, discuss the following questions:**

● **How was this activity like or unlike praying?**

● **Do you listen to God? What have you heard?**

● **What interferes with your ability to concentrate on hearing God's Word?**

● **What's one thing you can do to increase your ability to concentrate on hearing God's Word?**

Say: **It's tough to concentrate on listening to someone else when a need of your own gets in the way—like the need to avoid frostbite!**

Ask pairs to form foursomes. Say: <u>**We need to focus on**</u>  <u>**God,**</u> **and the Bible describes a spiritual discipline that can help us do that. It's called fasting. Fasting is abstaining from eating food, and some brief fasts have included abstaining from both eating and drinking water—though such fasts are rare.**

Say: **Fasting isn't an eating disorder. Fasting is choosing not to**

LEADER TIP
for Staying Focused

If the number of kids in your group prevents the easy formation of foursomes, select trios or pairs. The purpose of working in four-somes is to encourage teenagers to form re-lationships other than those they're already comfortable in.

eat in order to focus on God. In your foursomes, let's examine several people in the Bible who fasted. Distribute a "Fast Fasting Facts" handout (p. 55) to each student, and ask teenagers to discuss the questions on the handouts.

Ask foursomes to report back to the group, giving an overview of their discussions and asking any unanswered questions. Say: **Fasting in itself isn't particularly virtuous. Nor is it particularly Christian. Muslims fast. Jews fast. Atheists fast.**

But fasting for the purposes of prayer and repentance can be powerful. Intellectually, it can clear our minds. Spiritually, it can help us listen and show us how <u>we need to focus on God</u>. And practically, it can clear away a host of details that can keep us from focusing on prayer.

LIFE APPLICATION ▼

Fasting for Fun and Profit (10 to 15 minutes)

Say: **Although <u>we need to focus on God</u>, some people misunderstand exactly how to do that. But God gives us several important insights into profitable fasting. Let's prepare to give advice to someone who is very proud of his ability to fast. Ladies and gentlemen, I ask for a volunteer.**

Wait until one steps forward; then with great applause usher the volunteer to the center of the room. Say: **Our volunteer will act out the part of a man once spotted on a busy downtown corner in Jesus' day.**

The rest of you must choose one of these three corners (indicate three corners of the room) **and walk to it now. Our Pharisee will stay here.**

Wait for teenagers to select a corner, then assign one of the following passages to each corner: Isaiah 1:13-14; Isaiah 58:6-7; and Matthew 6:16.

Have your volunteer act out the role of the Pharisee as you say: **The man is a Pharisee. He's dressed in rich clothing. He's good-looking, healthy, and obviously successful. The Pharisee glances around to make sure he has an audience, then he lifts his head and begins to pray, "God, I thank you that I am not like all other men—robbers, evildoers, adulterers...I fast twice a week and give a tenth of all I get" (Luke 18:11b-12).**

Ask each group to select a spokesperson, read its passage, then agree on what advice to give the Pharisee about spiritually profitable fasting—if the Pharisee is interested in listening!

After each spokesperson has summarized his or her group's passage, ask the Pharisee if he (or she) wishes to respond. Then ask the larger group to discuss these questions:

● **Does this seem like good advice to you? Why or why not?**

● **Does this advice apply to our Pharisee friend? Why or why not?**

● **Does this advice apply to us? Why or why not?**

Cross Search (10 to 15 minutes)

Say: **Field trip! Pair up with someone you've not been in a group with yet, and make sure at least one of you has a watch. If your pair doesn't have a watch, please recruit one from a pair that has two.**

Distribute a piece of paper and a pencil to each pair. Say: **Your assignment is to find as many crosses as possible in five minutes. When you see one, briefly describe it on your piece of paper. Be creative! A telephone pole is a cross; so is your partner if his or her arms are outstretched. Remember that you must be back in five minutes or less. Ready? Go!**

LEADER TIP for Cross Search

Before you send your teenagers careening around the building, clearly state the rules and guidelines about where they may go... and how loud they may be. Avoid disturbing other groups or leaving the option open of dashing across the street to Burger-in-a-Bag to look for crosses in a jumbo order of french fries.

"Is not this the kind of **fasting** I have chosen:

to loose the chains of injustice and untie the cords of the yoke, to set the oppressed free and break every yoke?

Is it not to share your food with the hungry and to provide the poor wanderer with shelter—when you see the naked, to clothe him, and **not to turn away** from your own flesh and blood?"

—Isaiah 58:6-7

When everyone has returned, ask pairs to total their number of "cross sightings." Ask pairs to name the crosses on their lists that are the largest, the smallest, the most unusual, the tallest, and in the most unlikely places. Ask pairs to look at their lists and nominate the one they consider the "weirdest." List nominees on a chalkboard or newsprint, and call for an all-group vote to select a winner.

As a group, discuss these questions:

● **What would happen if every time we saw something that reminded us of a cross, we briefly focused on God and prayed?**

● **How many times a day would you pray?**

● **How do you think that would change your life?**

After your teenagers respond, say: **I'd like a volunteer to read aloud a quick message from the Apostle Paul.** Ask the volunteer to read aloud Ephesians 6:18.

Say: **Paul isn't suggesting that we live every moment with our heads bowed and our hands folded. He's talking about living our lives knowing that <u>we need to focus on God</u> and being ready to pray at all times. Developing a relationship with God includes a natural habit of praying for extended periods of time as well as sharing quick prayers—maybe each time we see a cross or each time we get in a car or each time we sit down to eat a meal. Turn to a partner, and share one trigger that would work for you—something that would prompt a quick prayer, a quick focus on God. Is it a cross or something else you see or do regularly throughout the day? And what would you pray for when you see or experience the prayer trigger?**

After teenagers have had time for their discussions, ask partners to pause to pray for each other. Then ask volunteers to talk about their triggers and what they'd pray for each time they see or experience them.

Say: **Great ideas! And I trust you'll put them into practice this week. Let's begin our habit of focusing on God by praying right now.**

CLOSING ▼

Our Father (5 to 10 minutes) Ask students to move a bit apart and settle themselves comfortably. Tell them they'll be joining you in prayer for five to ten minutes. They may sit, stand, kneel, or lie down. Play a cassette tape or CD of soft, instrumental music. Note the time you actually begin praying so you'll be able to tell teenagers how long they prayed when you've finished.

Explain: **A "directed prayer" is one in which a leader suggests topics for you to pray about. I'll ask you to silently pray about something. After a few moments, I'll ask you to pray about something else.**

We'll pray about topics suggested by the Lord's Prayer in Matthew 6:9b-13 (New King James Version). **I know many of you**

memorized this prayer years ago, but don't jump ahead of me as we pray together.

Get comfortable. Close your eyes, and please join me in prayer.

"Our Father in heaven,"

Not all of us completely respect our earthly fathers. Some of us may not live with them or see them regularly. But God, you are a Father who knows, loves, and never leaves us.

Tell God what you expect from him as your Father. Is it love? acceptance? Share those thoughts with your Father.

"hallowed be Your name."

Hallowed, holy, sacred—you are high above us, God, and worthy of our praise.

Praise God for his might and purity, his holiness. Thank him for preparing a place for you in heaven. What might that place be like?

"Your kingdom come."

You are our king, Lord. We are your servants. But how well have we served you, Lord? Help us see ourselves as you see us.

Think about ways you have served and ways you have failed to serve—at home, at school, and in relationships.

"Your will be done on earth as it is in heaven."

How can we be part of your will, Lord? What would you have us do?

Think about how you can carry out God's will.

"Give us this day our daily bread."

Remove from us all worry about the future, God. Give us an assurance that in you we have all we need. Give us peace, Lord.

Express to the Lord your worries.

"And forgive us our debts, as we forgive our debtors."

God, do you *mean* what you say here? That you'll forgive us in the same way, to the same measure, that we forgive others? How well do we forgive others, God? Bring to each of our minds one person we need to forgive.

Pray now for that person.

"And do not lead us into temptation, but deliver us from the evil one."

Thank you for being the light in a dark world, God. We trust you. We tell you the truth, God, because you are truth.

Confess to God one temptation you seem unable to resist. Perhaps it's a temptation to be impure in thought or deed, to lie, to be proud, to gossip, or to steal from God by misusing your time or money. Whatever it is, confess this temptation now.

"For Yours is the kingdom and the power and the glory forever."

Give us hearts for your kingdom, God. Help us see others in the same way you see them. Bring to our minds people we need to love who are at school, at home, and in our own group.

Pray for those in need of your love.

"Amen."

When you've finished praying, note how long this activity lasted, and say: **You have just prayed for** [disclose the amount of time]. **That's longer than many of you have prayed in weeks. When you fast, you'll find your ability to concentrate on prayer grows—that's just one of the benefits of fasting.** Close by having students form pairs and discuss with their partners ways they can encourage each other to pray regularly during the upcoming week.

DEPTHFINDER — FASTING WITH CARE

Caution! Fasting is physically beneficial to most people. But there are exceptions, including young children, the elderly, diabetics, women who are pregnant or nursing, and other people with specific medical problems. If there is any question about the advisability of going without food, consult a doctor before fasting.

Also be sure your students aren't using fasting to mask serious eating disorders such as anorexia or bulimia. For more information on discussing eating disorders with your students, see the Core Belief Bible Study "Suitable for Framing" from *The Truth About Creation*, Group Publishing, Inc., 1997, and *The Thin Disguise*, Thomas Nelson Publishers, 1996.

Among the benefits of fasting are an increased ability to concentrate, a sharpening of the mind, and a general cleansing of the body. But before you decide to fast as a group, make sure you get permission from parents and guardians.

FAST

Fasting Facts

In your group, look up and read the following passages. Be prepared to answer these questions:

● Who was fasting and for how long?

● What was the purpose of the fast?

● Do you think the person fasted for a good reason?

● Could you do what the person did?

Joshua 7:2-7

2 SAMUEL 12:13-20

Nehemiah 1:1-4

Daniel 10:1-3

Matthew 4:1-2

why ▼ Active and Interactive Learning works with teenagers

Let's Start With the Big Picture

Think back to a major life lesson you've learned.

Got it? Now answer these questions:

● Did you learn your lesson from something you read?

● Did you learn it from something you heard?

● Did you learn it from something you experienced?

If you're like 99 percent of your peers, you answered "yes" only to the third question—you learned your life lesson from something you experienced.

This simple test illustrates the most convincing reason for using active and interactive learning with young people: People learn best through experience. Or to put it even more simply, people learn by doing.

Learning by doing is what active learning is all about. No more sitting quietly in chairs and listening to a speaker expound theories about God—that's passive learning. Active learning gets kids out of their chairs and into the experience of life. With active learning, kids get to *do* what they're studying. They *feel* the effects of the principles you teach. They *learn* by experiencing truth firsthand.

Active learning works because it recognizes three basic learning needs and uses them in concert to enable young people to make discoveries on their own and to find practical life applications for the truths they believe.

So what are these three basic learning needs?

1. Teenagers need action.

2. Teenagers need to think.

3. Teenagers need to talk.

Read on to find out exactly how these needs will be met by using the active and interactive learning techniques in Group's Core Belief Bible Study Series in your youth group.

1. Teenagers Need Action

Aircraft pilots know well the difference between passive and active learning. Their passive learning comes through listening to flight instructors and reading flight-instruction books. Their active learning comes through actually flying an airplane or flight simulator. Books and lectures may be helpful, but pilots really learn to fly by manipulating a plane's controls themselves.

We can help young people learn in a similar way. Though we may engage students passively in some reading and listening to teachers, their understanding and application of God's Word will really take off through simulated and real-life experiences.

Forms of active learning include simulation games; role-plays; service projects; experiments; research projects; group pantomimes; mock trials; construction projects; purposeful games; field trips; and, of course, the most powerful form of active learning—real-life experiences.

We can more fully explain active learning by exploring four of its characteristics:

● **Active learning is an adventure.** Passive learning is almost always predictable. Students sit passively while the teacher or speaker follows a planned outline or script.

In active learning, kids may learn lessons the teacher never envisioned. Because the leader trusts students to help create the learning experience, learners may venture into unforeseen discoveries. And often the teacher learns as much as the students.

● **Active learning is fun and captivating.** What are we communicating when we say, "OK, the fun's over—time to talk about God"? What's the hidden message? That joy is separate from God? And that learning is separate from joy?

What a shame.

Active learning is not joyless. One seventh-grader we interviewed clearly remembered her best Sunday school lesson: "Jesus was the light, and we went into a dark room and shut off the lights. We had a candle, and we learned that Jesus is the light and the dark can't shut off the light." That's active learning. Deena enjoyed the lesson. She had fun. And she learned.

Active learning intrigues people. Whether they find a foot-washing experience captivating or maybe a bit uncomfortable, they learn. And they learn on a level deeper than any work sheet or teacher's lecture could ever reach.

● **Active learning involves everyone.** Here the difference between passive and active learning becomes abundantly clear. It's like the difference between watching a football game on television and actually playing in the game.

The "trust walk" provides a good example of involving everyone in active learning. Half of the group members put on blindfolds; the other half serve as guides. The "blind" people trust the guides to lead them through the building or outdoors. The guides prevent the blind people from falling down stairs or tripping over rocks. Everyone needs to participate to learn the inherent lessons of trust, faith, doubt, fear, confidence, and servanthood. Passive spectators of this experience would learn little, but participants learn a great deal.

● **Active learning is focused through debriefing.** Activity simply for activity's sake doesn't usually result in good learning. Debriefing— evaluating an experience by discussing it in pairs or small groups— helps focus the experience and draw out its meaning. Debriefing helps sort and order the information students gather during the experience. It helps learners relate the recently experienced activity to their lives.

The process of debriefing is best started immediately after an experience. We use a three-step process in debriefing: reflection, interpretation, and application.

Reflection—This first step asks the students, "How did you feel?" Active-learning experiences typically evoke an emotional reaction, so it's appropriate to begin debriefing at that level.

Some people ask, "What do feelings have to do with education?" Feelings have everything to do with education. Think back again to that time in your life when you learned a big lesson. In all likelihood, strong feelings accompanied that lesson. Our emotions tend to cement things into our memories.

When you're debriefing, use open-ended questions to probe feelings. Avoid questions that can be answered with a "yes" or "no." Let your learners know that there are no wrong answers to these "feeling" questions. Everyone's feelings are valid.

Interpretation—The next step in the debriefing process asks, "What does this mean to you? How is this experience like or unlike some other aspect of your life?" Now you're asking people to identify a message or principle from the experience.

You want your learners to discover the message for themselves. So instead of telling students your answers, take the time to ask questions that encourage self-discovery. Use Scripture and discussion in pairs or small groups to explore how the actions and effects of the activity might translate to their lives.

Alert! Some of your people may interpret wonderful messages that you never intended. That's not failure! That's the Holy Spirit at work. God allows us to catch different glimpses of his kingdom even when we all look through the same glass.

Application—The final debriefing step asks, "What will you do about it?" This step moves learning into action. Your young people have shared a common experience. They've discovered a principle. Now they must create something new with what they've just experienced and interpreted. They must integrate the message into their lives.

The application stage of debriefing calls for a decision. Ask your students how they'll change, how they'll grow, what they'll do as a result of your time together.

2. Teenagers Need to Think

Today's students have been trained not to think. They aren't dumber than previous generations. We've simply conditioned them not to use their heads.

You see, we've trained our kids to respond with the simplistic answers they think the teacher wants to hear. Fill-in-the-blank student workbooks and teachers who ask dead-end questions such as "What's the capital of Delaware?" have produced kids and adults who have learned not to think.

And it doesn't just happen in junior high or high school. Our children are schooled very early not to think. Teachers attempt to help kids read with nonsensical fill-in-the-blank drills, word scrambles, and missing-letter puzzles.

Helping teenagers think requires a paradigm shift in how we teach. We need to plan for and set aside time for higher-order thinking and be willing to reduce our time spent on lower-order parroting. Group's Core Belief Bible Study Series is designed to help you do just that.

Thinking classrooms look quite different from traditional classrooms. In most church environments, the teacher does most of the talking and hopes that knowledge will transmit from his or her brain to the students'. In thinking settings, the teacher coaches students to ponder, wonder, imagine, and problem-solve.

3. Teenagers Need to Talk

Everyone knows that the person who learns the most in any class is the teacher. Explaining a concept to someone else is usually more helpful to the explainer than to the listener. So why not let the students do more teaching? That's one of the chief benefits of letting kids do the talking. This process is called interactive learning.

What is interactive learning? Interactive learning occurs when students discuss and work cooperatively in pairs or small groups.

Interactive learning encourages learners to work together. It honors the fact that students can learn from one another, not just from the teacher. Students work together in pairs or small groups to accomplish shared goals. They build together, discuss together, and present together. They teach each other and learn from one another. Success as a group is celebrated. Positive interdependence promotes individual and group learning.

Interactive learning not only helps people learn but also helps learners feel better about themselves and get along better with others. It accomplishes these things more effectively than the independent or competitive methods.

Here's a selection of interactive learning techniques that are used in Group's Core Belief Bible Study Series. With any of these models, leaders may assign students to specific partners or small groups. This will maximize cooperation and learning by preventing all the "rowdies" from linking up. And it will allow for new friendships to form outside of established cliques.

Following any period of partner or small-group work, the leader may reconvene the entire class for large-group processing. During this time the teacher may ask for reports or discoveries from individuals or teams. This technique builds in accountability for the teacherless pairs and small groups.

Pair-Share—With this technique each student turns to a partner and responds to a question or problem from the teacher or leader. Every learner responds. There are no passive observers. The teacher may then ask people to share their partners' responses.

Study Partners—Most curricula and most teachers call for Scripture passages to be read to the whole class by one person. One reads; the others doze.

Why not relinquish some teacher control and let partners read and react with each other? They'll all be involved—and will learn more.

Learning Groups—Students work together in small groups to create a model, design artwork, or study a passage or story; then they discuss what they learned through the experience. Each person in the learning group may be assigned a specific role. Here are some examples:

Reader

Recorder (makes notes of key thoughts expressed during the reading or discussion)

Checker (makes sure everyone understands and agrees with answers arrived at by the group)

Encourager (urges silent members to share their thoughts)

When everyone has a specific responsibility, knows what it is, and contributes to a small group, much is accomplished and much is learned.

Summary Partners—One student reads a paragraph, then the partner summarizes the paragraph or interprets its meaning. Partners alternate roles with each paragraph.

The paraphrasing technique also works well in discussions. Anyone who wishes to share a thought must first paraphrase what the previous person said. This sharpens listening skills and demonstrates the power of feedback communication.

Jigsaw—Each person in a small group examines a different concept, Scripture, or part of an issue. Then each teaches the others in the group. Thus, all members teach, and all must learn the others' discoveries. This technique is called a jigsaw because individuals are responsible to their group for different pieces of the puzzle.

JIGSAW EXAMPLE

Here's an example of a jigsaw.

Assign four-person teams. Have teammates each number off from one to four. Have all the Ones go to one corner of the room, all the Twos to another corner, and so on.

Tell team members they're responsible for learning information in their numbered corners and then for teaching their team members when they return to their original teams.

Give the following assignments to various groups:

Ones: Read Psalm 22. Discuss and list the prophecies made about Jesus.

Twos: Read Isaiah 52:13–53:12. Discuss and list the prophecies made about Jesus.

Threes: Read Matthew 27:1-32. Discuss and list the things that happened to Jesus.

Fours: Read Matthew 27:33-66. Discuss and list the things that happened to Jesus.

After the corner groups meet and discuss, instruct all learners to return to their original teams and report what they've learned. Then have each team determine which prophecies about Jesus were fulfilled in the passages from Matthew.

Call on various individuals in each team to report one or two prophecies that were fulfilled.

You Can Do It Too!

All this information may sound revolutionary to you, but it's really not. God has been using active and interactive learning to teach his people for generations. Just look at Abraham and Isaac, Jacob and Esau, Moses and the Israelites, Ruth and Boaz. And then there's Jesus, who used active learning all the time!

Group's Core Belief Bible Study Series makes it easy for you to use active and interactive learning with your group. The active and interactive elements are automatically built in! Just follow the outlines, and watch as your kids grow through experience and positive interaction with others.

FOR DEEPER STUDY

For more information on incorporating active and interactive learning into your work with teenagers, check out these resources:

● *Why Nobody Learns Much of Anything at Church: And How to Fix It,* by Thom and Joani Schultz (Group Publishing) and
● *Do It! Active Learning in Youth Ministry,* by Thom and Joani Schultz (Group Publishing).

your evaluation of

Bible Study Series
for senior high

why PRAYER matters

Group Publishing, Inc.
Attention: Core Belief Talk-Back
P.O. Box 481
Loveland, CO 80539
Fax: (970) 669-1994

Please help us continue to provide innovative and useful resources for ministry. After you've led the studies in this volume, take a moment to fill out this evaluation; then mail or fax it to us at the address above. Thanks!

● ● ● ● ● ●

1. As a whole, this book has been (circle one)

not very helpful   very helpful
1   2   3   4   5   6   7   8   9   10

2. The best things about this book:

3. How this book could be improved:

4. What I will change because of this book:

5. Would you be interested in field-testing future Core Belief Bible Studies and giving us your feedback? If so, please complete the information below:

Name _____

Street address _____

City _____ State _____ Zip _____

Daytime telephone (____) _____ Date _____

THANKS!